Original title:
Concrete Dreams

Copyright © 2024 Creative Arts Management OÜ
All rights reserved.

Author: Thor Castlebury
ISBN HARDBACK: 978-9916-88-062-3
ISBN PAPERBACK: 978-9916-88-063-0

Urban Whispers

In the alleys where shadows play,
Soft murmurs dance and sway.
Neon lights flicker bright,
Guiding dreams through the night.

Pavement stories, untold cries,
Hidden tales beneath the skies.
A heartbeat echoes, clear and low,
As city souls wander to and fro.

Steel Shadows at Dusk

Tall buildings scrape the evening light,
Casting shadows, deep and slight.
Steel and glass in a silent race,
Embracing dusk's gentle embrace.

Beneath the sky's fading hue,
Life unfolds, ever new.
In the hush, a whispering breeze,
Promises linger, hearts at ease.

Echoes of the Cityscape

Footsteps linger on cobblestone,
Remnants of lives, all alone.
Echoes of laughter, close and far,
Mark the moments beneath the stars.

In the noise, a melody plays,
Cycles of night melt into day.
Voices weaving through the air,
Stories woven with utmost care.

Dreams in Glass and Steel

Reflections shimmer in the glass,
Capturing time as moments pass.
Steel frames rise against the sky,
Whispers of dreams that dare to fly.

In this maze of work and play,
Hope ignites, guiding the way.
The city's pulse beats like a drum,
A symphony of all that's to come.

Echos in the Infrastructures

Concrete whispers in the night,
Steel beams hold tales of flight.
Footsteps linger, shadows blend,
Silent stories without end.

Overhead, the sirens wail,
Stories woven, a hidden trail.
Glimmers of life in the seams,
Every corner holds our dreams.

Distant Chimes in the City

A clock tower standing bold,
Chiming softly, tales retold.
Horns of buses, voices rise,
City's heart beneath the skies.

In the distance, laughter sings,
Echoes of old, new beginnings.
Each note carries through the air,
A melody rich and rare.

Graffiti's Silent Lullaby

Colors dance upon the walls,
Hidden truths as evening falls.
Spray cans whisper, stories told,
Art in shadows, bold yet cold.

Each stroke breathes life to the street,
Silent lullabies bittersweet.
Voices trapped in vibrant hues,
Echoing dreams, hopes, and views.

Neon Dreams and Alleyways

Neon lights flicker and play,
Guiding the lost, come what may.
Alleyways hold secrets tight,
Beneath the glow of urban light.

Footsteps echo, a fleeting sound,
Hungry dreams in shadows found.
Whispers of lives intertwined,
In this city, peace you'll find.

Fragments of Twilight

The day fades gently, colors blend,
Whispers of night begin to send.
Stars awaken, small and bright,
In the silence, dreams take flight.

Shadows stretch beneath the trees,
A soft breeze carries memories.
Echoes linger, softly play,
In twilight's arms, the world will sway.

Fleeting moments lost in time,
Captured softly, like a rhyme.
Nature sighs as lights grow dim,
In this dusk, our hopes swim.

Time stands still, as night draws near,
Every heartbeat, calm and clear.
Fragments of a day gone by,
In twilight's grace, we learn to fly.

Where Pavement Meets Sky

Concrete rivers, urban flow,
In the city's pulse, life will grow.
Skyward dreams with buildings high,
Where the pavement meets the sky.

Voices echo, stories share,
Life unfolds with vibrant flair.
Hands reach out for what is near,
In this chaos, beauty's clear.

Sunrise paints the streets anew,
Golden hues in morning dew.
Every shadow tells a tale,
In this city, we set sail.

Clouds drift lazily above,
As we wander, lost in love.
Where the pavement meets the sky,
Endless hopes and dreams can fly.

Beneath Urban Canopies

Beneath the trees, a soft embrace,
Whispers linger in this space.
Leaves flutter, stories told,
In the heart of green, we behold.

City life hums all around,
Yet here in quiet, peace is found.
Footsteps soften on the ground,
In this refuge, joy is crowned.

Sunlight dapples through the leaves,
Nature's art in which we believe.
A moment's pause in hectic days,
Beneath urban canopies, we praise.

Fresh scents of earth, a gentle sigh,
In this haven, spirits fly.
With every breath, the world feels new,
Beneath the trees, our dreams break through.

Urban Echoes

In crowded streets, the voices blend,
A symphony that never ends.
Each heartbeat in the bustling throng,
An urban echo, fierce and strong.

Footsteps hurry, time won't wait,
Stories woven, intertwining fate.
Lost in haze or found in light,
In the city, day turns night.

Graffiti speaks on crumbling walls,
Whispers of passion in the calls.
Artistry in every space,
Urban echoes leave their trace.

In this maze of steel and stone,
Together, yet we feel alone.
Yet every echo softly chimes,
In urban hearts, we find the rhymes.

Concrete Gardens of Tomorrow

In shadows of towers, dreams find their place,
Whispers of green in a cold, hard space.
Seeds of resilience pushed through concrete,
Hope blooms in cracks where the earth and sky meet.

Each flower a story of struggle and strife,
Nurtured by sunlight, they dance back to life.
A testament living where few dare to tread,
Concrete gardens, where the brave hearts are led.

Steel and Solitude

Under the skyline, a lone figure stands,
Steel beams embrace the dreams in their hands.
Echoes of footsteps on asphalt paths worn,
Silence surrounds, yet a new day is born.

The breeze carries whispers of hopes left behind,
In shadows of factories, the weary unwind.
Finding connection in spaces so vast,
Steel and solitude, in visions contrast.

Urban Dandelions Growing Wild

Among the tall buildings, yellow blooms rise,
Against the concrete, they stretch for the skies.
Dandelions dancing with the winds of change,
Urban resilience in a world so strange.

They thrive in the cracks, where few ever stare,
Nature's defiance in the heart of despair.
Each puff of their seeds carries whispers of free,
Urban dandelions, wild and carefree.

City Lights and Heartbeats

City lights flicker like stars in the night,
Illuminating dreams, making shadows take flight.
Heartbeats synchronize with the rhythm of cars,
Each pulse a reminder that we carry our scars.

In bustling avenues, hope sculpts our way,
Moments of magic in the dusk and the day.
Under the glow, we find warmth in the sight,
City lights spark anew, igniting our light.

Beneath the Surface

In the depths where silence hums,
Whispers flow like gentle drums.
Hidden truths in shadows sleep,
Secrets buried, buried deep.

Through the murmur of the tide,
Feel the world's soft pulse inside.
Rippling tales of love and strife,
Tangled knots of hidden life.

Bubbles dance in fleeting light,
Echoes of a muted night.
When the water's still and clear,
What lies beneath will appear.

Cityscapes of the Soul

Streets alive with dreams untold,
Among the bricks, hearts unfold.
Neon signs and shadows blend,
Every corner has a friend.

Skyscrapers scrape the endless blue,
Whispers of hope in every hue.
Voices rise in a pulsing beat,
Life dances on urban feet.

In alleyways where echoes play,
Fragments of lives drift and sway.
City lights like stars at night,
Guide our souls toward the light.

When Towers Touch the Sky

Steel giants reaching so high,
Kissing clouds as dreams fly by.
In the shadows, stories dwell,
Of every heart that dared to swell.

Windows reflect the world outside,
In their glass, hopes cannot hide.
With every floor, ambition climbs,
Rising up to greet the times.

Voices echo in the breeze,
Within the heights, we find our keys.
Together we strive, together we sigh,
For we are one when towers touch the sky.

Graffiti of Memories

On concrete walls, our voices scream,
Colors burst like a waking dream.
Every stroke, a story told,
Memories cherished, never old.

Spray paint whispers of our past,
In vibrant hues, our shadows cast.
Laughter, pain, in every line,
A gallery where hearts entwine.

Time is fleeting, yet we remain,
In these murals, joy and pain.
A tapestry of life so bold,
Graffiti sings of what we hold.

Nightfall Over Metropolis

The city hums, a gentle sigh,
As shadows blend with the twilight sky.
Skyscrapers loom like giants tall,
Whispers echo in the urban sprawl.

Stars emerge, a flickering dance,
While streetlights cast a fleeting glance.
The asphalt glistens, slick and bright,
Night unveils a different sight.

Voices fade, a soft farewell,
In the stillness, secrets dwell.
Moonlight drapes the world in grace,
Night invites us to embrace.

Dreams awaken, softly tread,
As hearts in darkness gently spread.
In this realm, we find our place,
Nightfall wraps us in its embrace.

The Pulse of Paved Streets

Footsteps echo, a rhythmic beat,
Concrete veins beneath our feet.
Every corner holds a tale,
In pavement's grace, we set our sail.

Cars rush by, a vibrant stream,
Life unfolds like a vivid dream.
The pulse of streets, alive and loud,
Among the rush, we feel so proud.

Voices mingle, laughter flares,
Moments shared in fleeting stares.
Each heartbeat thumps, the city thrives,
In tangled paths, our spirit dives.

As the sun sets, shadows blend,
In urban hearts, friendships mend.
Paved streets carry us along,
In their rhythm, we find our song.

Asphalt Reveries

Beneath our feet, the asphalt dreams,
Whispers of life in silver beams.
The world above, a flickering glow,
While hidden stories ebb and flow.

Graffiti speaks of hopes and fears,
Urban tales that pierce our gears.
Each crack a memory, worn yet sweet,
Where strangers meet and futures greet.

Footprints linger, traces left,
In this canvas, we are deft.
The heart of asphalt beats in time,
A timeless dance, a silent rhyme.

In every shadowed alleyway,
Dreams collide and drift away.
We wander through these reveries,
Asphalt binding our memories.

Neon Hues and Forgotten Views

Neon flashes, bold and bright,
Painting stories in the night.
Lost in hues of electric flare,
We walk through magic, unaware.

Billboards shout in vibrant hue,
While echoes of silence break through.
Forgotten views in glimmers speak,
In every corner, visions peek.

Flickers of joy, whispers of pain,
Life unfolds like summer rain.
In neon glow, past meets the now,
A reminder of what we allow.

Time drifts softly, moments blend,
In neon dreams, we start to mend.
With each pulse of light, we live,
Eternal dance in what we give.

Hopes Etched in Cement

In streets where dreams align,
Whispers of the past incline.
Marks of love, where we once stood,
Imprints of a heart, so good.

Time drifts like clouds in flight,
Chasing shadows, seeking light.
Every crack tells a story,
A silent song of faded glory.

Beneath the weight, we still aspire,
With gentle strength, we never tire.
In every chip, a wish remains,
Hope is etched, in joy and pains.

Together we shall rise anew,
From hardened ground, to skies so blue.
Each step forward, we'll embrace,
Dreams that time cannot erase.

Serenity in the Sidewalk Cracks

Among the stones, green breaks through,
Nature's grace in shades of dew.
Gentle blooms in concrete's breath,
A quiet dance, defying death.

In stillness found in bustling roads,
Life persists, despite the loads.
Cracks may mar the path we tread,
Yet beauty springs where hope is fed.

Through chaos, peace finds its spark,
In faded lines, a soothing mark.
Resilience sings in whispers sweet,
In sidewalk cracks, our hearts meet.

Nature's art in urban wear,
Serenity woven with care.
Life unfolds in soft embrace,
In every crack, a sacred space.

Rain on Rooftops

Drumming softly on tin and slate,
Melodies that soothe and create.
Each drop a note, pure and clear,
A symphony for all who hear.

Puddles form where dreams can swim,
Reflections dance, the edges trim.
Clouds embrace the earth below,
In whispered tales, they ebb and flow.

Footsteps splash on cobblestones,
Every heartbeat, a gentle tone.
The world awash in silver gray,
Rain brings peace, washes fears away.

In moments still, a quiet pause,
Nature's touch, it gives us cause.
Under rooftops, we find our way,
In rain's embrace, we learn to stay.

Strangers Beneath Neon Lights

In a city where shadows play,
Neon signs light the way.
Lost souls wander streets unknown,
In every corner, dreams are sown.

Glances shared in fleeting time,
Silent stories intertwined.
Echoes of laughter fill the air,
In the night, we find a prayer.

Beneath the glow of vibrant hues,
Faith in strangers feels like news.
Connections bloom, however brief,
In fleeting moments, we find relief.

Together in the electric night,
We chase our hopes, we seek the light.
In busy streets, hearts unify,
Beneath neon lights, we learn to fly.

City Skies in Twilight

The sun dips low in the embrace,
Casting hues of pink and gold,
Buildings stand as silent guards,
Whispering tales of dreams untold.

A canvas stretched, the night unfolds,
Stars peek through as shadows play,
Traffic lights begin to blink,
A symphony of the close of day.

Breezes carry scents of life,
Laughter dances in the air,
Hope ignites in twilight's charm,
City souls are free, laid bare.

As the world begins to sleep,
The skyline glimmers, soft and bright,
In the heart of urban rhythms,
A magic found in fading light.

Dreams Beneath Skyscrapers

Beneath the towers touching sky,
Dreams flutter like leaves in breeze,
Voices murmur, hopes take flight,
In shadows deep, hearts find ease.

Concrete gardens of bright desires,
Where souls wander, lost and found,
Echoes of laughter fill the streets,
Resonating, a gentle sound.

Daylight dims, and stars awake,
Chasing wishes, bold and new,
Skyscrapers loom, yet hearts unite,
In every shade, in every hue.

Stories linger in alleyways,
Life unfolds in vibrant streams,
Beneath the weight of steel and glass,
We weave the fabric of our dreams.

Shadows on Asphalt

Silent footsteps on the road,
Shadows stretch in evening's arms,
City whispers call our names,
In asphalt's grip, we find our charms.

Neon lights flicker like stars,
Traffic flows like restless tide,
In the pulse of urban life,
Our secrets in the dark we hide.

Alleyways whisper old stories,
As evening air wraps us tight,
We chase the flicker of our dreams,
In shadows born of fading light.

Moments captured, fleeting time,
The world's heartbeat, slow and fast,
Shadows dance on urban streets,
In every step, we leave our past.

Echoes of the Urban Heart

In the city's breath, we linger,
Echoes pulse in every beat,
Brick and stone, our silent choir,
Life swells in the rhythm of feet.

The skyline hums a lullaby,
As headlights spark against the night,
Every corner holds a heartbeat,
A tapestry of dreams takes flight.

Beneath the glow of streetlamps,
Voices meld in soft refrain,
The urban heart is wild and free,
Each story shared, a drop of rain.

In midnight's hush, we come alive,
Connecting threads of joy and pain,
The city's echo sings to us,
In the heart's embrace, we remain.

Dreaming in Concrete

In the city where shadows play,
Hustle whispers night and day.
Concrete skies above so gray,
Yet dreams find light in fading ray.

Through the cracks, a flower grows,
Hope resides where no one knows.
A tapestry where each thread shows,
The beauty in the heart it chose.

Winds of change brush past the walls,
Echoes of life in empty halls.
Within this maze, a spirit calls,
To dance amidst the city's thralls.

Here we weave our stories bold,
In every stone, a dream retold.
Amidst the grey, a heart of gold,
In concrete dreams, our lives unfold.

A Symphony of Graffiti

Colors clash in vibrant hues,
On brick canvases, stories fuse.
Each spray, a voice that seeks to choose,
A symphony the heart can use.

Whispers painted on the street,
Rhythms echo, pulses beat.
Every corner, a tale discreet,
In the art, strangers meet.

A dance of chaos, wild and free,
Each stroke a note in harmony.
From the underground, a decree,
Art shall rise, unbound and glee.

Together, they weave night and day,
Through vibrant sprays, the souls relay.
In graffiti's grasp, we find a way,
To meld our hearts, a grand ballet.

Whispers of the Shattered Pavement

Cracked and worn, the pavement sighs,
Beneath our feet, the city cries.
Stories buried in broken ties,
Each step we take, a chance to rise.

Whispers carried on the breeze,
Lost dreams hidden in the leaves.
In every fault, a memory weaves,
A fragile dance as time deceives.

Ghosts of laughter, echoes fade,
Memories in the shadows laid.
Life moves on, yet still we wade,
Through the tales that the ground displayed.

In each crack, a tale is spun,
Heartbeats mingle, past and done.
Together here, we are all one,
In shattered pavements, life's begun.

Heartstrings in the Concrete Jungle

Deep in the jungle, iron and stone,
Heartstrings pull, pulling us home.
Among the chaos, seeds are sown,
In this city, we're never alone.

Towers rise toward the sky,
While dreams soar, unable to fly.
Through the maze, we laugh and cry,
In each heartbeat, the reason why.

Streetlights flicker, a guiding star,
Each shadow hides a life, a scar.
Weaving stories, no matter how far,
In concrete jungles, we raise the bar.

Together we stand, hearts intertwined,
In this urban symphony, love defined.
Every step a new tale aligned,
In the concrete jungle, hope enshrined.

Architecture of Longing

In shadows cast by dreams at night,
Walls adorned with whispers tight.
Each corner holds a silent plea,
A yearning call to be set free.

Windows frame the starlit sky,
Embers flicker, softly sigh.
Foundation strong, yet hearts can sway,
In longing's maze, we lose our way.

Cement blooms where echoes fade,
Every step, a choice we've made.
Within these halls, desire thrives,
As hope and memory collide.

Brick by brick, the tale unfolds,
A story of the brave and bold.
In this design, our souls entwine,
Each longing wish a sacred sign.

The Symmetry of Solace

In tranquil spaces, silence reigns,
Where symmetry breaks worldly chains.
Each line and curve, a gentle grace,
In solace found, our fears erase.

Mirrored souls reflect the calm,
Balancing chaos with a psalm.
Through arches high and shadows low,
A harmony begins to grow.

Columns stand as guardians bold,
Holding stories yet untold.
In every pause, a breath of peace,
In geometries, our troubles cease.

To seek the beauty in the real,
In crafted forms, our hearts can heal.
With each embrace of shape and space,
We find a truth, a warm embrace.

Urban Reveries

Beneath the hum of bustling streets,
A patchwork quilt where life competes.
Skyscrapers pierce the vibrant sky,
In urban dreams, our spirits fly.

Neon lights paint the night's soft edge,
As whispers echo from each ledge.
In crowded spaces, solitude grows,
A dance of faces, the ebb and flows.

Graffiti blooms on concrete walls,
Tales of love where heartbeats call.
In alleys dark, the shadows play,
As midnight strokes the end of day.

Through every pulse of city life,
We weave our hopes amidst the strife.
In reveries, our dreams take flight,
Within this canvas, we ignite.

Steel and Stone Whispers

Amidst the clash of steel and stone,
Old tales linger, softly grown.
Every beam a story told,
In whispered truths, the past unfolds.

Rusty fixtures, weathered grace,
Time and toil carve each embrace.
In the creak of beams, we find our place,
Within the space, a warm embrace.

Bridges arch like dreams in flight,
Connecting worlds in day and night.
In every step on cobbled way,
The echoes of our yesterdays.

Through tangled roots and iron frames,
The heart remembers all our names.
In whispered winds through cracks and seams,
We listen close to our forgotten dreams.

Beneath the Towers

In shadows cast by iron heights,
Whispers of dreams take their flight.
Concrete giants, they stand so tall,
Yet in their shadows, we feel so small.

City life buzzes, bright and loud,
Hopes and fears entwined in a crowd.
Secrets hidden in alleyways deep,
Beneath the towers, the city dreams sleep.

Neon lights blink, guiding the way,
The night alive, in dance it sways.
Beneath the towers, where stories collide,
We find our path, let our hearts be our guide.

From dawn to dusk, the city's pulse beats,
In every corner, life quietly greets.
Beneath the towers, where life dares to soar,
We find our truth, forever wanting more.

Above the Clouds

In realms where silence drapes the sky,
Dreams take flight, like birds up high.
Soft, white blankets cradle the sun,
Above the clouds, life's race is won.

The world below, a distant hum,
Here, thoughts unravel, clarity comes.
Weightless wonders grace the blue,
Above the clouds, we see what's true.

A painter's brush, with strokes of light,
Colors dance in the soft twilight.
Above the clouds, where feelings bloom,
We find ourselves, dispelling gloom.

In the stillness, our spirits soar,
Finding peace, forevermore.
Above the clouds, dreams intertwine,
In this sanctuary, love is divine.

Metropolis of the Mind's Eye

A labyrinth forged from thoughts and dreams,
Endless streets flow like winding streams.
In the shadows, visions reside,
Metropolis vast, where secrets hide.

Echoes of laughter, whispers of fears,
Building memories through all the years.
Every corner, a story to tell,
In this realm, we know all too well.

Colors swirl in a breathtaking dance,
Wisps of time coax us to glance.
Metropolis vibrant, alive and bright,
In the mind's eye, it takes flight.

Across the skyline, dreams intertwine,
Crafting futures, both yours and mine.
In this city, our spirits ascend,
Metropolis of thoughts, where journeys blend.

Dreaming in a Cacophony of Sirens

In the night, the sirens call,
Their wails echo, a haunting thrall.
City lights flicker, casting shadows,
Dreams collide where chaos flows.

Amidst the noise, a heartbeat fast,
Whispers of pain, shadows are cast.
Yet in those cries, a spark ignites,
Hope and despair dance through the nights.

Dreamers wander, seeking the peace,
In a world where sounds never cease.
Within the cacophony, visions bloom,
In the dissonance, we find our room.

Through every siren's piercing song,
We rise up, resilient, strong.
In the depths of the night's dismay,
Dreaming brightly, we find our way.

Solace Found in Steel Frames

Amidst the grit, beneath the haze,
Steel frames rise, in countless ways.
A refuge crafted from strength and grace,
In their shadows, we find our place.

Life pulses through the structured flow,
In every beam, possibilities grow.
Solace found in the sturdy design,
A fortress against the tangled vine.

Windows wide open to the sky,
Letting dreams and hopes drift by.
In steel frames, our spirits unite,
Together we shine, even in night.

Rooted in strength, we build anew,
In every challenge, our courage grew.
Solace found where the world made strives,
In steel frames, the heart truly thrives.

Skyscraper Serenade

City lights shimmer, bright and bold,
Dreams entwined in stories untold.
Metal giants claw at the sky,
Whispers of hope in the night lie.

Elevators hum a soft tune,
Rising as fast as the waning moon.
Concrete heartbeats pulse with grace,
Fleeting moments, a hurried race.

Windows alive with flickering glow,
Silent songs of those down below.
Each floor a tale, a life on display,
Skyscrapers sing as night turns to day.

Amongst the steel, dreams take their flight,
Elevated wonders, kissing the light.
In this serenade, we all belong,
Under the stars, where we sing our song.

Shadows Beneath the Overpass

Lurking whispers in the dimly lit space,
Shadows stretch, intertwining with grace.
Concrete giants tower above,
Echoes of stories, lost without love.

Graffiti murals tell tales of the night,
Colors of dreams in a world lost to spite.
Beneath the arch, the lost wander by,
Silent reflections where hopes go to die.

Footsteps shuffle on pavement worn thin,
Flickering lights, where darkness has been.
Each echo a heartbeat, a cry for the past,
In the stillness, memories forever last.

Embrace the shadows, a shelter so deep,
Secrets they hold, in silence they keep.
Life pauses here, in the stories we weave,
Beneath the overpass, where we grieve.

Reflections in Rain Puddles

Raindrops dance on the pavement's skin,
Mirrored moments where dreams begin.
Puddles collect the sky's gray sighs,
Capturing echoes of fleeting goodbyes.

Each ripple tells a tale once told,
Fractured glimmers of silver and gold.
Nature's palette in vibrant hues,
Paints emotions, both old and new.

Barefoot wanderers splash with glee,
Lost in the magic, wild and free.
Reflections shimmer with every stride,
In each small world, a secret to hide.

As dusk whispers its lullaby soft,
Puddles glow gently, dreams lift aloft.
In rainy moments, we find our peace,
Through reflections, our worries cease.

Skyline by Moonlight

Crescent moon hangs, calm in the night,
Casting whispers of soft silver light.
Skyline dances, silhouettes bold,
A canvas of stories, waiting to unfold.

Stars twinkle gently, a guiding embrace,
Rooftops stretch high, reaching for space.
Night air hums with secrets untold,
In every shadow, a dream to hold.

Breezes carry the scent of the sea,
Windows aglow, alive with glee.
The horizon beckons, a siren's call,
Under the moon, we rise and we fall.

In this moment, the skyline's alive,
A testament found in the night we thrive.
With every breath, under starlit skies,
The heartbeat of cities, where magic lies.

Metamorphosis of the Heartstone

Deep within the cavern's glow,
A heartstone waits, its light aglow.
With whispers soft, it starts to change,
Emerging new, it feels so strange.

From hardened shell to vibrant hue,
It pulses like a dream come true.
Each beat a tale of love and pain,
Transforming scars into bright gain.

In shadows cast, the echoes dance,
The heartstone sways, it takes a chance.
With every breath, it learns to soar,
Breaking limits, seeking more.

Embrace the shift, the vivid spark,
In every heart lies a hidden mark.
Through trials faced, it claims its part,
The wondrous journey of the heart.

Pathways of Imagination

Winding trails in the mind's expanse,
Where thoughts like wildflowers dance.
Each twist and turn, a story told,
A canvas bright, a future bold.

In twilight realms where dreams unite,
Illusions glow with silver light.
Each pathway leads to secret lands,
Crafted by hope's gentle hands.

Through forests thick with whispered lore,
And rivers wide that long to explore.
With every step, new wonders grow,
Each journey sparks a vibrant glow.

So take a breath, begin to roam,
Let imagination guide you home.
Within each heart, a map resides,
To worlds unseen, where magic hides.

Skyline Veils of Hope

Above the city, stars align,
With wishes cast, both yours and mine.
The skyline glows like dreams asleep,
In veils of hope, our secrets keep.

Clouds drift softly, stories weave,
In every heart, the chance to believe.
Through trials faced, we rise anew,
With skies of blue, our spirits flew.

Each dawn that breaks, a promise made,
As shadows fade, our fears evade.
The horizon calls, a bright embrace,
Where courage blooms in open space.

So hold the sky, let dreams unfold,
In every heart, a tale retold.
With veils of hope, we start to climb,
To touch the stars, to dance with time.

Grains of Time in the City

In the hustle, whispers fade,
Footsteps mark the endless parade.
Stories written on pavement grey,
Grains of time slip quietly away.

Bricks and mortar hold their ground,
Echoes linger, a haunting sound.
Lost moments beneath the bright lights,
Memories weave through endless nights.

Each turn finds a piece of lore,
Life unfolds, forevermore.
In every shadow, a truth will stay,
Grains of time, in the city's sway.

Beneath the stars, the city dreams,
Lost in the flow of silver streams.
Caught in the moment, we hope to find,
The essence of life, unconfined.

Dust and Dreams

In corners dark, the shadows play,
Dust settles where memories lay.
Dreams once bold, now whispers faint,
A faded canvas, an artist's paint.

Beneath the layers, stories hide,
Of lives lived boldly, frail with pride.
Dust drifts slowly, a gentle sigh,
While dreams take wing, and dare to fly.

Each grain tells of love and loss,
Paths crossed once, now a silent gloss.
Echoes chase the light of day,
Dust and dreams in disarray.

Awake the heart, stir the past,
In every moment, find joy vast.
For in the dust, the dreams entwined,
Hold the essence of mankind.

Windows to the Soul of the City

Through glass and frame, we catch a glance,
Each window tells a tale of chance.
Life unfolds in colors bright,
Reflections dance in morning light.

Faces pass, each with a story,
Moments shared, no need for glory.
Inside they dream, while outside rush,
The pulse of life, in every hush.

In every pane, a glimpse we steal,
Conversations lost, yet so surreal.
Windows open, hearts explore,
The city's soul, forevermore.

Let us look deeper, beyond the view,
What stories wait, what lives are true?
In the frame of each day anew,
Windows to the heart, ever blue.

Skylines of the Forgotten

Silhouettes rise against the dusk,
Ghostly towers shrouded in rust.
Whispers echo through the night,
Skylines lost to fading light.

Once they stood proud, the dreams they held,
In each brick, a story spelled.
Forgotten lives beneath the stars,
Memories linger, left with scars.

Windows broken, no longer bright,
The past lingers, an aching sight.
Through time they stand, still and tall,
A tribute to those who gave their all.

In shadows deep, the spirits roam,
Seeking peace in a distant home.
Skylines tell what we ignore,
The forgotten dreams of days of yore.

Beneath the Urban Canopy

Steel towers loom high,
Casting shadows long,
Among the whispered streets,
Life hums its silent song.

Pavements cracked and worn,
Footsteps echo soft,
Stories intertwine here,
In each daydream loft.

Lush trees poke through stone,
Roots searching for light,
In this bustling realm,
Nature's gentle fight.

Hope blooms through the cracks,
Resilience on display,
Beneath the urban canopy,
Life finds its own way.

Solitary Figures at Dusk

Silhouettes at twilight,
Chasing fading light,
Whispers of the night,
In shadows out of sight.

Lonely streets begin,
To embrace the calm,
Fleeting moments pass,
In dusk's tender balm.

A figure stands alone,
Eyes lost in the haze,
Searching for a spark,
In the evening's maze.

The city breathes deep,
As stars start to gleam,
In the hush of dusk,
We weave our dream.

Bridges Between Dreams

Suspended in the air,
A bridge of fleeting hopes,
Crossing realms of wonder,
Where imagination copes.

Threads of gold and silver,
Connect each distant shore,
In the heart of longing,
We find forevermore.

Two souls reach across,
With whispers on the breeze,
Building trust and faith,
As they share their dreams with ease.

Together they will rise,
Above the clouds of doubt,
On bridges made of dreams,
What life is all about.

Urban Landscape of Yearning

Skyscrapers touch the sky,
A maze of hopes and fears,
Glistening in the dusk,
As each soul disappears.

Windows like deep oceans,
Reflective, vast, and wide,
Behind each pane of glass,
A thousand dreams reside.

The hum of city life,
Echoes through the night,
Yearning fills the air,
For stars just out of sight.

Beneath the urban glow,
Our hearts beat on the ground,
In this landscape of yearning,
Hope is always found.

Mosaic of Urban Life

In crowded streets, the faces blend,
Colors of struggle, hope, and mend.
A laughter echoes, memories shared,
In every corner, stories dared.

Neon lights flicker, dreams ignite,
Fragments of joy in the endless night.
Children play with hearts so free,
Amidst the rush, they just want to be.

Skyscrapers rise, touching the stars,
Yet shadows linger from old scars.
From the roof, we witness the whole,
A vibrant tapestry of soul.

In every crevice, life's pulse strong,
A world composed of right and wrong.
Together we dance, in pain and cheer,
Mosaic of life, forever here.

Skylines of Despair

Concrete giants scrape the sky,
Beneath their weight, the dreams can die.
Whispers of sorrow linger near,
In the silence, screams disappear.

Hope is hard to find in gray,
Lost among the streets of clay.
A flicker of light, a distant call,
Yet shadows loom, a heavy pall.

Once vibrant corners now feel bare,
Echoes of laughter lost in air.
The skyline weeps, a fractured heart,
Yearning for peace, a brand-new start.

Each soul a story, hidden deep,
In the city's arms, we seldom sleep.
Yet somewhere sparks of life ignite,
Skylines of despair can find the light.

Urban Canvases

Brick walls sing of colors bold,
Murals painted, stories told.
Each spray of paint, a voice to speak,
In the silence, art feels sleek.

Footsteps echo on the stone,
In every place, art feels at home.
Shapes of struggle, beauty too,
A canvas wide, for me and you.

Sidewalks paved with dreams unmet,
Artistry thrives, no regret.
In the alleys, find the truth,
Brush strokes dance, our shared youth.

Each corner whispers tales untold,
On urban canvases, hearts unfold.
A masterpiece, alive and free,
Painting the city's memory.

Whirlwind of Heartbeats

In the rush of life, we collide,
Every heartbeat, a place to hide.
City streets pulse, alive with sound,
In this whirlwind, truth is found.

Footsteps quicken on the ground,
In each moment, a life profound.
From dawn to dusk, the rhythm flows,
A myriad of tales, and it shows.

In crowded trains, strangers glance,
Connected souls in fleeting dance.
A heartbeat shared, a glance that stays,
In this tempest, we find our ways.

Life's whirlpool spins, yet we remain,
Chasing dreams caught in the rain.
In every heart, a song to sing,
A whirlwind of heartbeats, life takes wing.

Urban Fantasies

Amidst the steel and glass, dreams arise,
Neon lights dance, painting the skies.
Whispers of hope in crowded streets,
Every heartbeat, the city greets.

Chasing shadows in twilight's embrace,
Street performers bring a vibrant grace.
Laughter echoes, stories unfold,
In urban corners, treasures are told.

Voices merge in a rhythmic beat,
A symphony bright, where strangers meet.
Lives intertwine in vivid flair,
Urban fantasies linger in the air.

Each corner turned holds a new surprise,
In every gaze, a world lies.
With every step, a chance to explore,
In this urban maze, we crave more.

Reflections in the Glass

Mirrored facades reflect the past,
Echoes of laughter, shadows cast.
Fractured images, stories combined,
In city lights, our paths aligned.

A fleeting glance through crystal walls,
Moments captured as twilight falls.
Lost in the shimmer of distant dreams,
Reality dances in fractured beams.

Each window holds a whispering tale,
Of love and loss, of ships that sail.
In silence, secrets linger and wait,
For wandering souls to contemplate.

Reflections shift with the setting sun,
In the city's heart, we come undone.
Through the glass, we find who we are,
Guided by light, like a wandering star.

The Pulse of Pavement

Beneath our feet, the city breathes,
A heartbeat strong that never leaves.
Sidewalks thrum with every stride,
In this urban rhythm, we confide.

Echoing footsteps, a timeless beat,
Where dreams collide and spirits meet.
Concrete jungles pulse with life,
Amidst the hustle, joy, and strife.

Traffic flows like veins in the street,
A vibrant song, a syncopated feat.
The siren's call, the tapping sound,
In the pulse of pavement, we're unbound.

Each moment cherished, each path entwined,
In the city's embrace, our souls aligned.
Through laughter and tears, we navigate,
The pulse of pavement helps us create.

Lost in the Urban Maze

A labyrinth of streets, I wander alone,
In alleyways where dreams have grown.
A map of memories, lost and found,
In the urban maze, where silence resounds.

Graffiti whispers on weathered walls,
Echoes of youth in forgotten halls.
Each twist and turn, a journey anew,
Discovering stories in every view.

Footsteps follow where shadows play,
In the city's pulse, I lose my way.
Yet in the chaos, peace takes flight,
In the urban maze, I find my light.

Cafes spill laughter into the street,
Hidden corners where strangers meet.
Lost and found, in a vibrant haze,
Together we thrive in the urban maze.

Lanterns in the Night

In the dark they softly glow,
Leading dreams where hope can flow.
Each flicker tells a whispered tale,
Guiding hearts through night's veil.

Stars above may twinkle bright,
But it's lanterns that shed light.
They shimmer on the quiet street,
A symphony of warmth and heat.

Beneath their glow, we find our way,
Chasing shadows that want to stay.
The night blooms with gentle grace,
As lanterns dance in their embrace.

Together we roam through the dark,
With every step, igniting a spark.
In the hush, our worries take flight,
Finding peace in lanterns of light.

Sidewalks of Hope

Each step on pavement tells a story,
Of dreams that rise and seek their glory.
Cracks beneath our feet are signs,
Of battles fought and fragile lines.

Children play, their laughter rings,
Bouncing high on hopeful wings.
Each corner holds a brand new chance,
A moment's pause, a fleeting dance.

Flower pots in windows bloom,
Erasing shadows, dispelling gloom.
A mural bright, a heart in reach,
Whispers of love the sidewalks teach.

As day turns to dusk and we roam,
These sidewalks whisper, 'You are home.'
With every footfall, hope ignites,
In the tapestry of city lights.

Heartbeats in the Alley

In the alley where secrets dwell,
With echoed heartbeats, stories tell.
Flickering lights cast shadows long,
In the silence, we feel so strong.

Whispers drift on cooler nights,
Like shooting stars in city lights.
Each heartbeat syncs with the unseen,
In this vivid urban dream.

Graffiti speaks of love and pain,
Artistry in each bold strain.
As footsteps echo soft and low,
In the alley, connections grow.

Together we stand, hand in hand,
Finding strength in this secret land.
With heartbeats loud in twilight's call,
We rise and shine, we'll never fall.

Skylight Serenade

Under the stars, a soft melody,
Whispers of dreams drift free and easy.
Skylights gleam like a thousand eyes,
Reflecting hopes that grasp the skies.

The moon hums gently in the night,
Casting shadows, soft and bright.
Each note carries a tender sound,
A serenade where love is found.

In the quiet, we close our eyes,
Feeling the rhythm as night complies.
A dance of visions in the air,
In this moment, we're free from care.

With skylights above, we find our song,
Notes that linger where we belong.
Together in this twilight's embrace,
A serenade, a heart's warm space.

Unseen Worlds in Plain Sight

In whispers faint, the streets awake,
A dance of shadows, a silent quake.
Beneath the surface, life does flow,
Unseen worlds in the urban glow.

The hawker calls with a sigh so deep,
Lost tales stir from the city's sleep.
Windows glimmer, secrets confined,
Echoes of dreams, entwined and blind.

A child's laughter on a sunlit lane,
A flicker of joy amidst the mundane.
Watch the petals fall from the tree,
In plain sight, the magic we see.

In every corner, a story resides,
Of love and loss, where hope abides.
Unseen worlds dance just out of view,
In the heart of the city, alive and true.

Symphony of the Sirens

Beneath the moon, the shadows sway,
Harsh cries of sirens lead the way.
A haunting tune in the night's embrace,
Whispers of stories across time and space.

Neon lights flicker like stars in flight,
Each echo carries a tale of the night.
A symphony born from chaos and strife,
Threads of existence, the pulse of life.

Lured by the sounds, lost souls convene,
In the city's heart, where dreams glean.
They dance in circles, both near and far,
Chasing the light of a distant star.

In tunes of steel and cries of despair,
A beauty lingers, beyond compare.
The symphony calls, a siren's song,
In the depths of our hearts, we all belong.

Skylines and Shadows

Concrete giants touch the sky,
Whispers of dreams as clouds float by.
Silhouettes cast on twilight's stage,
In every corner, a new age.

The skyline flares at the break of dawn,
With hopes reborn, old fears withdrawn.
The dance of lights, a vibrant thrill,
Embracing the silence, the world stands still.

Beyond glass towers, a tale unfolds,
Street artists paint where the magic molds.
Each stroke tells of the lives they've met,
A canvas alive, with no regret.

In shadows deep, where mysteries lie,
Bound by the dreams that never die.
Skylines whisper their age-old charms,
In the urban pulse, we find our arms.

Urban Mystique

Amidst the hustle, a secret breathes,
Hidden in alleys where the night weaves.
Banners sway in the evening breeze,
Capturing whispers of thoughts that tease.

Among the rush, stillness ignites,
Stories glimmer in urban lights.
The rhythm of life beats fierce and strong,
In the heart of the city, where we belong.

Concrete jungles, a tapestry spun,
Threads of struggle, threads of fun.
Where dreamers gather, and legends bloom,
In the urban mystique, we find our room.

From rooftops high to the pavements low,
The city thrives, an endless flow.
In every heartbeat, a truth we seek,
In urban dreams, the soul finds its peak.

Asphalt Serenades

In the city's heart, dreams collide,
Footfalls echo, nowhere to hide.
Neon lights flicker, shadows dance,
Each step a story, lost in a trance.

Underneath the night's embrace,
Whispers linger, time leaves a trace.
Pavement cracks tell tales of old,
Silent secrets, brave and bold.

Cars rush by, a fleeting glance,
Life moves fast, no second chance.
Yet within the chaos, music flows,
Asphalt serenades, the city knows.

Every corner holds a sigh,
In the distance, a lullaby.
Worn-out souls find solace here,
In the city's song, they disappear.

Footsteps in Forgotten Places

Amidst the ruins, shadows creep,
Footsteps echo, memories seep.
Time stands still in quiet halls,
Whispers linger, history calls.

Dusty books and silent chairs,
Ghostly laughter fills the air.
Windows broken, curtains torn,
Life once thrived, now hope is worn.

A faded photograph, a tale untold,
Love and loss in frames of old.
Nature healing, reclaiming space,
Footsteps linger in forgotten places.

Beneath the weight of shifting earth,
Echoes resonate with untold worth.
In every corner, a soul embraces,
The magic found in forgotten places.

Sunsets behind Steel

Beneath giants of iron and glass,
The sun dips low, a moment to pass.
Colors bleed in the evening sky,
As day whispers its last goodbye.

Shadows stretch on the city floor,
A canvas painted, forever more.
Steel beams glint in the twilight warm,
The horizon cradles the day's charm.

Hope flickers in the fading light,
As dreams awaken to embrace the night.
Concrete jungles hum a tune,
While stars emerge to greet the moon.

In the heart of chaos, beauty thrives,
Sunsets behind steel, where magic arrives.
With every glow, a promise unfolds,
Of whispered stories, waiting to be told.

Labyrinth of the Lost

Winding pathways, lost in thought,
In shadows deep, lessons taught.
Every turn a memory found,
In silence deep, their voices sound.

Twisting halls where echoes weave,
The fragile hopes that we believe.
Flickering lights, they guide the way,
Through tangled dreams that choose to stay.

Labyrinths of heart and mind,
Within the maze, the truth we find.
Whispers call from corners near,
The path ahead becomes more clear.

Though lost we walk, we are not alone,
In the labyrinth's depths, we find our home.
With every step, we draw the cost,
In the journey's heart, we are never lost.

Hearts Unveiled by Moonlight

Underneath the silver glow,
Two souls whisper secrets low.
Silence hums, a gentle tune,
Hearts unveiled beneath the moon.

Starlit skies their witness stand,
Fingers clasped, a lover's hand.
Mirrored dreams in twilight's sheen,
Love awakened, soft and keen.

Gentle breezes weave a spell,
In this night, all is well.
Every glance, a silent vow,
Forever starts with here and now.

As the night begins to fade,
Morning light, their serenade.
Hearts still beat in perfect rhyme,
Together through the sands of time.

Murmurs of the Midnight City

Neon lights flicker and dance,
Whispers echo, a fleeting chance.
Sidewalks pulse with restless beats,
In the crowd, a heart retreats.

Voices blend, a symphony,
Lost in dreams, we'll set them free.
City breathes a lullaby,
Underneath the midnight sky.

Shadows drape the alley walls,
In the silence, the laughter calls.
Every corner, a story kept,
In the night, memories slept.

Through the maze of hopes and fears,
Life unfurls like whispered cheers.
For in the city's vibrant heart,
Each moment is a work of art.

Dreams on the Edge of Pavement

Bare feet dance on asphalt dreams,
Where the streetlight softly beams.
Each crack holds a tale untold,
A world of wonder to behold.

Colors splash in twilight's sway,
Fading thoughts of yesterday.
Voices rise with the evening sun,
A chorus bright, a race begun.

In the rush, time slips away,
Moments weave, then they fray.
Yet here we chase the fleeting light,
With laughter echoing through the night.

Endless possibilities ignite,
Paths we wander in pure delight.
On the edge where dreams take flight,
Life unfolds in colorful sight.

Forgotten Stories of Stone

Ancient walls whisper their lore,
Echoing voices from before.
Stone by stone, the tales reside,
In the shadows, where secrets hide.

Moss-covered paths, the timeworn trails,
Memories linger in the gales.
Each brick a chapter, worn but proud,
A testament, silent yet loud.

Through storms and sun, they stand so tall,
Holding stories, the rise and fall.
Legends carved in weathered grain,
In the echo of loss and gain.

Listen closely, and you may find,
The voices of the past entwined.
For every stone has lived and grown,
In forgotten tales, we find our own.

The Rhythm of the Pavement

Footsteps echo, a dance of the street,
Concrete beats under weary feet.
City symphony, a bustling song,
In every heart, the pulse is strong.

Skyscrapers rise, shadows entwined,
Whispers of dreams, a world unconfined.
Windows flicker, stories unfold,
In every corner, a life to behold.

The hustle, the flow, a vibrant sea,
In every soul, a yearning to be free.
As day turns to night, the lights ignite,
The rhythm of the pavement feels just right.

With each heartbeat, the city breathes,
In the cracks of the pavement, hope weaves.
Stories linger where footsteps tread,
In the city's pulse, the dreams are fed.

Hopes in Urban Ruins

Once grand structures now fade away,
Echoes of laughter, in shadows they play.
Graffiti whispers on crumbling walls,
Bright colors blooming in concrete halls.

Reclaimed by nature, the vines do climb,
A silent witness to the march of time.
Yet in the decay, new life will sprout,
From cinders of past, new dreams come about.

Forgotten places hold tales untold,
Of love and loss, and courage bold.
Amidst the ruins, resilience grows,
In every crack, possibility flows.

Fading memories, yet still they inspire,
In the heart of the lost, an unyielding fire.
Urban ruins, where hopes intertwine,
Crafting new futures, they quietly shine.

Graffiti Dreams on Brick Walls

Splash of colors ignites the grey,
Voices of youth in bold array.
Stories etched on the city's face,
In every stroke, a vibrant trace.

Walls whisper secrets, dreams take flight,
Mural artists paint the night.
Echoes of feelings, hearts laid bare,
In this urban canvas, art does share.

Spray cans dance beneath the moon,
Urban rhythms create a tune.
From the shadows, a cry for change,
In every pigment, the world's rearranged.

Graffiti dreams, a powerful voice,
In a world of chaos, they find their choice.
On brick walls, hope forever sprawls,
A testament to life, in vivid thralls.

Forgotten Alleyways of the Mind

In quiet corners where shadows dwell,
Whispers echo, secrets to tell.
Thoughts meander like lost streams,
In the alleyways, we chase our dreams.

Memories linger, both bitter and sweet,
Forgotten laughter, faded heartbeat.
Paths of reflection, a winding maze,
In the darkest corners, the bright flame stays.

Lost in reverie, time drifts away,
In the alleys of thought, night turns to day.
Every twist leads to the past,
In moments of silence, the die is cast.

Through the fog of nostalgia, we quietly roam,
Each step we take, we carry our home.
Forgotten alleyways, both refuge and bind,
In shadows and light, we search and find.

Nighttime Narratives

In shadows cast by the moon's silver light,
Whispers of secrets dance in the night.
Stars are the storytellers, silent and still,
Each twinkle a tale, each glimmer a thrill.

Under the heavens, the world holds its breath,
Embracing the magic, defying all death.
Dreams wander softly, through darkened skies,
Nighttime unfolds, where imagination flies.

The clock ticks slowly, as time takes a pause,
Nature's sweet lullaby, with gentle applause.
A symphony woven with crickets and breeze,
In this twilight realm, the heart finds its ease.

As dawn approaches, the stories may fade,
Yet memories linger, in shadows they've laid.
The night cradles whispers that time cannot steal,
A canvas of dreams, painted with zeal.

Steel Roots and Dreams

Amidst the concrete, dreams take their flight,
Metal and ambition, shining so bright.
Skyscrapers rise, where shadows once dwelled,
Steel roots grip the earth, as stories are held.

Workers unite, hands calloused and worn,
Building tomorrow, from the ashes of dawn.
Each rivet a promise, each beam a new hope,
Through struggles and triumphs, together they cope.

In alleyways hidden, hearts start to soar,
Voices of youth, forever exploring.
Painting the city with colors of dreams,
As steel roots embrace, or so it seems.

From every corner, aspirations arise,
A tapestry woven beneath urban skies.
Steel roots intertwine, with spirit so bold,
In the heart of the city, stories unfold.

Beneath the Streetlight Glow

Beneath the soft halo, the world seems at rest,
Streetlights keep watch, like guardians blessed.
Whispers of lovers, lost in their gaze,
Moments entwined in a delicate haze.

Echoes of footsteps on pavement so worn,
Reminding us all of the dreams we adorn.
The glow paints the shadows, a gentle embrace,
In this fleeting moment, we find our true place.

With each flickering bulb, a story to share,
A meeting of souls, a moment laid bare.
Under the starlight, where the city ignites,
Hope lingers softly in the still of the nights.

As dawn's first light chases the darkness away,
The echoes grow faint, but the magic will stay.
For beneath every streetlight, memories flow,
A night of connection, beneath the glow.

Transience in the Terrazzo

On floors of terrazzo, stories do gleam,
Fragments of journeys, like dreams in a dream.
Each colorful shard tells a life once lived,
In patterns of love, loss, and the gifts we've received.

Footsteps upon paths that have weathered the years,
Echoing laughter, and sometimes the tears.
The mosaic whispers of times long ago,
In colors and shapes, through the ebb and the flow.

As sunlight cascades, it dances with grace,
Illuminating memories, etched in their space.
Transience captured, yet somehow it stays,
In the heart of the terrazzo, throughout all our days.

The beauty of fleeting, the charm of unknown,
In every reflection, we're never alone.
Our lives intertwine, like the stones in a row,
Finding forever in moments that glow.

The Weight of Urban Epiphanies

In shadowed corners thoughts collide,
A million stories, worlds reside.
Concrete giants hug the sky,
We grasp at dreams that wander by.

Neon glows, a fleeting muse,
Moments seized and quick to lose.
Amid the noise, a silent plea,
The heart beats loud, yet yearns to flee.

Each step a dance on weathered stone,
In every crack, a life once known.
Lives intertwined in fleeting sights,
Epiphanies found in city nights.

But in this maze we often roam,
We find in chaos, we find a home.
A canvas vast, we'll paint with care,
The weight we carry, light as air.

Whirling Through the Grit

Dust and dreams like whispers swirl,
In the city's chaos, we unfurl.
Spirals of thought in fevered chase,
Tangled moments, a wild embrace.

Graffiti speaks on tired walls,
Echoes of laughter in crowded halls.
A rhythm born of vibrant strife,
Whirling through the grit of life.

Traffic hums a restless tune,
Beneath the watch of a silver moon.
Life's pulse quickens, heart on fire,
In the street's embrace, we find desire.

Through alleys dark and avenues bright,
In every turn, a flicker of light.
We dance with shadows, laugh and cry,
In the grit of the city, we learn to fly.

Beneath the Surface of City Breath

Beneath the pulse, a secret thrum,
City breathes, a quiet hum.
In alleyways where silence dwells,
Whispers tell of ancient spells.

Pavement cracks with tales untold,
In every stone, a history bold.
Veins of asphalt, rivers of light,
The city awakens, day turns to night.

Underneath the rush, we sense,
A sacred space, alive, intense.
Hearts beat softly in the crowd,
A tapestry of dreams, proud and loud.

With every breath, the city sighs,
In every corner, a new surprise.
Together we weave through joys and fears,
Beneath the surface, life appears.

Lost in the Labyrinth of Streets

Wanderer lost in echoes bright,
Paths uncertain in morning light.
Each corner turned, a choice to make,
In the labyrinth, dreams awake.

Mosaic pieces underfoot,
Footsteps dance where roots take root.
Voices blend in a marbled haze,
Guiding hearts in tangled ways.

Over bridges, under skies,
City breathes with no goodbyes.
Each step, a story unfolds,
Treasures hidden, mysteries hold.

Yet in the maze where shadows play,
We find our truths along the way.
In every turn, there's space to grow,
Lost in streets, we learn to know.